Water World

Precious McKenzie

ROURKE PUBLISHING

www.rourkepublishing.com

www.rourkepublishing.com

PHOTO CREDITS: Cover: © Dim154; Title Page: © Blojfo; Page 4: © Jan Rysavy; Page 5: © Shupian; Page 6: © Sergei Popov, © Lukasz Gonerski; Page 7: © Dannyphoto80; Page 8: © Juergen Sack; Page 9: © Graham Prentice; Page 10: © Alex Gulevich; Page 11: © Lee Torrens; Page 12 © Gary Blakeley; Page 13 © Ivan Bajic, Ari Sanjaya, Lisegagne; Page 14: © Lisa Thornberg; Page 15: © Peter Leahy, Albert kok: Wikipedia, Tommy Schultz, stphillips; Page 16: © Wikipedia, NOAA, Davidyoung11111, Luna Vandoorne Vallejo, Page 17: © Darren Bradley; Page 18: © US Fish & Wildlife; Page 19: © US Coast Guard; Page 20: © Rechitan Sorin; Page 21: © Enrico Fianchini, © Rocio Veltman; Page 22: © Hughstoneian

Edited by Meg Greve

Cover and Interior design by Tara Raymo

Library of Congress Cataloging-in-Publication Data

McKenzie, Precious
  Water World / Precious McKenzie.
    p. cm. -- (Green Earth Science Discovery Library)
  Includes bibliographical references and index.
  ISBN 978-1-61741-769-6 (hard cover) (alk. paper)
  ISBN 978-1-61741-971-3 (soft cover)
  Library of Congress Control Number: 2011924815

Rourke Publishing
Printed in the United States of America, North Mankato, Minnesota
060711
060711CL

www.rourkepublishing.com - rourke@rourkepublishing.com
Post Office Box 643328 Vero Beach, Florida 32964

Table of Contents

The Water Cycle

Did you know that more than 71 percent of the Earth's surface is water?

Without water there would be no life on Earth.

Humans, plants, and animals need water to stay alive.

Where does all of this water come from?
Water falls to Earth as snow or rain. Water
collects in lakes, rivers, and oceans.

Water Cycle

Condensation

Precipitation

Evaporation

Runoff

In Our Homes

We depend on water every day. We drink it, cook with it, and bathe in it.

Workers at water treatment facilities clean and treat water so that it is safe for us to use.

Water and Work

Farmers use water to help grow crops. They also use water for their livestock to drink.

If there is a **drought**, farmers may not have enough water for their animals and crops.

We use the water in oceans and rivers to move **freight** and people. Ocean liners carry products all over the world.

We can buy toys from China, chocolate from Africa, and coffee from South America.

North America

Europe

Asia

Africa

South America

Australia

Antarctica

The world's oceans and rivers are also full of fish. They provide food for many people.

Atlantic Grouper

Clown Fish

Smallfish Sawtooth

Some species of fish are endangered because of **overfishing**.

15

Life in the Water

Large animals like whales and **microscopic** creatures like zooplankton live in water. Every plant and animal has an important role in the food web.

Aquatic plants protect small marine animals. Larger fish or animals eat the smaller animals and plants.

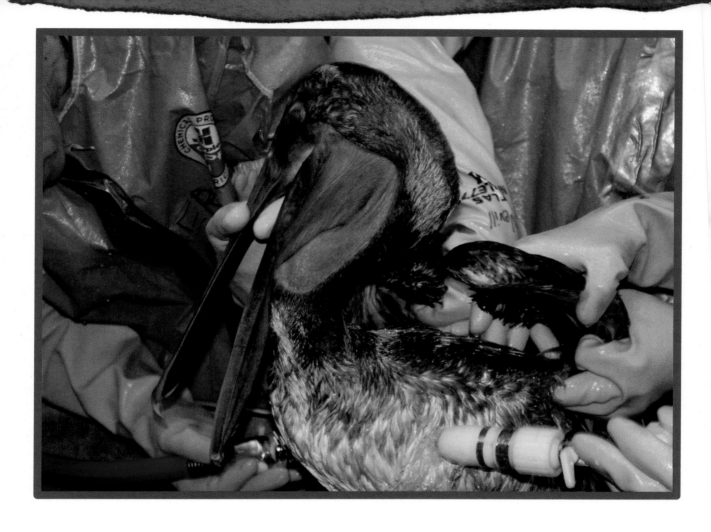

Life depends on water. Disasters such as oil spills, litter, and human waste **pollute** our waterways.

The oil slick from this explosion covered more than 4,000 miles (6,437 kilometers) of ocean water.

In 2010, an offshore oil drilling rig, the Deepwater Horizon, exploded in the Gulf of Mexico.

Doing Our Part

We can do our part to clean and protect our watery world.

Keep pesticides and other harmful chemica out of waterways.

Put trash in containers, not in the water or along the shoreline.

Volunteer in coastal clean-up efforts.

There are billions of people in the world. We all need water. You can help **conserve** water and protect our beautiful watery world!

Try This

Turn off the water while you brush your teeth. You'll be surprised at how much water your entire family can save!

Glossary

aquatic (uh-KWAT-ik): something that lives or grows in water

conserve (kuhn-SURV): to save from waste or loss

drought (DROUT): a period of time when there is little or no rain

freight (FRAYT): products carried by ships, trucks, or trains to places where it will be sold

microscopic (mye-kruh-SKOP-ik): so small that it can only be seen with a microscope

overfishing (OH-vur-FISH-ing): the act of catching a number of fish that harms a fish population or a habitat

pollute (puh-LOOT): to make dirty with trash or chemicals

Index

Websites

www.kids.nationalgeographic.com

www.exploretheblue.discoveryeducation.com

www.liveblueinitiative.org

About the Author

Precious McKenzie lives in Florida with her husband, three children, and two dogs. She writes books for children and teaches English at the University of South Florida. In her free time, she enjoys being outside hiking and swimming.